STORY STRUCTURE

STEP-BY-STEP

Essential Story Building, Story Development and Suspense Writing Tricks Any Writer Can Learn

Sandy Marsh

Table of Contents

Introduction

Thank you and congratulations on purchasing *"Story Structure: Step-by-Step | Essential Story Building, Story Development and Suspense Writing Tricks Any Writer Can Learn"*.

This book was created to help you learn a series of tips and tricks that will help you enrich your story and make it a must-read book for your target audience. By using these techniques and strategies in your own book you will be able to generate a storyline that is rich with suspense, action, and other tools that are important to keep your readers engaged and excited about reading your book.

Each chapter within' this book is dedicated to one element of story structures themselves, ensuring that you are provided with the greatest in-depth detail to ensure that you learn plenty to help you produce a phenomenal story. Before the book ends, you will be provided with tips from top writers and authors that will help you write like the pros.

This book was not designed for any particular experience level when it comes to writing. Instead, it has been populated with tricks that will help any writer from beginner to advanced. If you are someone who typically struggles to write stories but you are looking to get yours heard, you can be certain that you will learn some tips here to help you get on your way towards having your book completed. Likewise, if you have done this before but are looking for a refresher or are otherwise interested in learning more to enrich your story and create an addictive read for your audience, you are certainly going to learn something also.

Please be sure to take your time and work through all of the tips and tricks provided within' this book. While some may not be entirely relevant to the work you are producing, they may provide you with inspiration to move forward in a more powerful way. As well, be sure to keep this book handy for future writing ventures as you never know which part will stand out each time. Finally, remember that writing is an experience that should be enjoyed by both the reader and the author. Be sure that you take the time to make the process enjoyable for yourself so that you can produce your best work. And finally, have fun!

Chapter 1: Purpose of Story Structure

Understanding the purpose of story structure will ensure that you are aware of how it can make (or break) your story, and why it is so crucial that you develop a strong structure within' your own story. Prior to diving into any important tips or strategies, we are going to explore what a story structure is, exactly, and what purpose it serves within' your story.

What is a Story Structure?

In basic form, a story structure is essentially a map that is drawn to take your reader from point a to point b. You want them to start at the beginning of the book and end at the end, only after being taken through an experience which is essentially each "stop" on the map. This map is used to help identify how people solve different problems, as well as to assist in conveying the message that the author is attempting to send from the storytelling process. In essence, the structure of your story is the process where the outline is transformed from being a simple idea to being the bones of your story. It becomes the part that holds the entire story up and gives it a form that is both natural, yet moving.

Where do Story Structures Come from?

Story structure is less of an invention or creation and more of an element of the story that was observed and thus plucked from the process and used as a tool to help generate new stories. For thousands of years, humans have been telling stories to one another whilst using story structure without ever knowing what it actually was. This is the part of the story that was used to draw listeners or readers forward through the story while keeping them actively engaged and wanting to know more. With the use of story structure, storytellers were able to walk people through the process of the story, rather than simply telling them the beginning and end factors. This meant that storytelling became an experience, both for the teller and the listener or reader. It was all thanks to story structure.

Although people weren't aware of what story structure actually was in the beginning, the idea of it emerged over time. It was identified as the structure of the story that was used to describe how certain characters within' the story dealt with problems and overcame them, as well as how they interacted with and communicated with other individuals from the story.

After identifying the concept of story structure and observing it from ancient storytelling experiences, people began using it as a general guideline for the process of building stories. Now, your story structure involves important information about the setting of your story, the people involved, the conflicts they experience, and how they overcome said conflicts. It is essentially every part of your story pulled together and planned out in a specific structure that helps you as the author understand what story you are trying to tell before and during the writing process.

Why You Need One

Having a story structure may seem pointless, especially if you already have the story in your head and you are simply attempting to get it out on paper. However, story structures are extremely valuable and can help you with the entire storytelling process. They are excellent for helping you identify how you are going to deliver the story to ensure that the reader receives the story effectively. This is more than simply providing the reader with information to help walk them from point a to point b. Instead, it is about giving them this relevant information in such a way that they are eager to know more and they stay actively engaged with the storytelling process.

When you design your story structure it helps you identify what your story sounds like to other people when they are reading it. It is important that you develop one before you start writing so that you have a strong execution plan going into the writing process. While you can simply write the story from your mind, this may result in you not emphasizing strong points enough, or otherwise diluting your story with information that takes away from it having a strong structure. Instead, you could plan your story out on paper first and essentially lay out the points that you will take your readers through within' the story. This way you can walk yourself through it and learn more about your story in advance. Doing this gives you the opportunity to identify any weak points and strengthen them, to ensure that your story makes sense and flows well, and to develop confidence in the idea that you have generated a strong enough plotline that your readers are going to stay actively engaged and enjoy the reading experience.

Now that you are more clear on what a story structure is and why it is so crucial to the writing process, it is time to explore the process of actually creating your own story structure so that you can embark on writing your own story. The following chapters will walk you through the step-by-step process of building your own story structure, as well as every technique you should know in order to have a strong structure that will leave your readers wanting more.

Chapter 2: The Essentials of Building a Structure

The first part of generating your own story structure is understanding the essentials. In this chapter, we are going to explore all of the basics that you should know when it comes to creating your own story structure. Throughout this chapter, you will be provided with tips and techniques to help you design the foundation of your structure. By the end, you should have a solid structure that will help you produce a phenomenal story.

9 Step Process

Most stories follow a typical nine-step process in order to generate their story structure. Some people prefer to alternate how the structure is designed, such as by introducing the climax in the first portion of the book. Still, they typically tend to break the book up into three main parts, or "acts" as they are called. This helps keep each part of the book focused on a certain subject that ultimately contributes to the overall story.

The following sections will introduce each step of the nine-step process and how they should be executed in order to produce a high-quality story structure. Please note that these are following the traditional method based on how many other stories have been structured throughout the ages. You may choose to alternate yours if you are more advanced, but if you are new to storytelling you will likely want to stick to and master this traditional structure before venturing into other structures. This will provide you with more practice towards developing a structure and using the purpose of the structure to your advantage. Once you are more skilled with structures then you can start to create alternative ones for your future stories because you will have a stronger idea about what makes them work and what doesn't.

Step One: First Act

The first step is to introduce the first act. This is the part of the story where you want to introduce the reader to your characters, the setting you have chosen, and anything that is at stake in the story. This is where they understand what is important and why. In the first act, you are given the opportunity to catch the attention of the reader and give them a reason to care about what story you are telling.

Example: You are writing a romance novel so you introduce the two lovers, as well as any other important characters to the reader. You will also take the time to provide insight as to where the book is taking place. This is where you can introduce the stakes as well, which essentially means you are telling the reader what is at stake and why it is important to the protagonist.

Step Two: The First Major Plot Point

The second step is to introduce the first major plot point to your reader. This should be defined by an event that takes place which forces the character to take action. You want this first major plot point to be considered the last scene in the first act so that readers are left wanting more. This is the finale of the first part of your book, so you want to leave it with some form of small cliffhanger. This both rewards the reader for reading by giving them some action to pay attention to, but also has them wondering what is going to come next as a result of the character's actions.

Example: The female character in your romance novel is walking home when an attacker tries to hurt her. The male character comes seemingly from nowhere and defends her honor, ensuring that she was protected and was not harmed by the attacker.

Step Three: First Half of Second Act

This is the part of the book where your character is coming back from the action they took at the end of the first act. Here you further explain what happened as a result of that plot point, as well as how your characters are dealing with it.

Example: As a result of him being the first to hit the attacker, despite him attempting to defend the female, the male role in your novel is being subjected to a criminal investigation. Because of this, he is trying to keep a low profile and avoid any further complications. The female is angry with the male for not calling the cops instead and allowing them to deal with it. She is upset that he has subjected himself to the criminal investigation through his actions, regardless of his reasoning.

Step Four: Second Major Plot Point

This is a plot point within' the story where the character who was attempting to regain their bearings from the first major plot point is forced back into action. Here, you want to work together with what said character has at stake to help the reader understand why they have been forced into action. Often the action is forced unto the character in the form of an ultimatum.

Example: Despite keeping a low profile for some time, the attacker returns and attempts to strike again. Only this time, he knows that the male is with the female and the attacker is attempting to force the male to act. He wants to have the male punished for attacking him, regardless of the fact that he was only attempting to protect her from the attacker. As a result, the male role is forced to decide between protecting her again or being faced with serious jail time. For the sake of these examples, let's say that he chooses to defend her honor once again.

Step Five: Second Half of Second Act

This is the part where all of the characters in the story begin to come into their own. Here, they are all grouping together to come against the antagonist. They are ensuring that the initial character is no longer left to take action on his or her own, but rather that they are supported by the other characters within' the story.

Example: This time, the female character is aware of what is going on and she is fighting to protect the male character. She is no longer angry with him for making the choice he made originally, and she is more willing to testify in his defense. They work together to get the attacker in trouble and to protect the male character through pleading that he was only practicing self-defense.

Step Six: Third Major Plot Point

This is where the protagonist's behavior appears to have led him or her to a place of defeat. In this part of the story, you want to introduce the idea that there may be no hope for this character and that they may be doomed because of the antagonistic forces. Here, they are beginning to feel as though they have hit rock bottom.

Example: Despite the female character testifying to the male character and fighting in his corner this time around, the court orders him guilty for assault. It appears that even though he was attempting to protect himself and the female character, no one is willing to see that. It seems there is no hope for him to avoid criminal charges altogether.

Step Seven: Third Act

In the third act, the protagonist is fighting against the antagonistic force as a last effort to take them down. Here they may not have total confidence that they can do it but they are not willing to give up just yet.

Example: The male character chooses to appeal the court ruling. Together, he and the female work to create a plan where they will prove that he is innocent and the attacker is the one who is truly guilty.

Step Eight: Climax

This is where there is a final face-off between the protagonist and antagonist. This is the deciding moment that is responsible for determining whether the story will end in favor of the antagonist, or in favor of the protagonist.

Example: The male character and the attacker face off in court. This is the part of the story that will determine whether the male is ruled guilty and is no longer welcome to appeal the charges, or whether the judge will see that he is actually innocent and it is the attacker who should be facing charges. For the sake of the example, we will say that it ends with the attacker being charged and the male being let off.

Step Nine: Resolution

This is where any loose ends from the story. It will also give insight to how the characters react to the climax and where they end up afterward. This is the wind down where readers are given the opportunity to know "what's next" and is required to avoid you from ending your book in a cliff-hanger.

Example: The female character is ecstatic that the male character is let free and they decide that they never want to risk facing a life without the other so they choose to get married.

As you can see, developing a strong story structure is important. Hopefully, through the use of the examples, you were able to understand how the structure lent a hand towards generating suspense and giving the reader a reason to keep reading. Because of how the story was structured and when certain pieces of information were revealed, the individual reading the story once it was complete would be engaged and would thus stay committed to reading the entire story so that they could discover how it ended.

It is important that you pay attention to the book in three sections as outlined above, as well as that you have a major plot point in each part. Dividing your story into three sections ensures that each part focuses on a particular element of the story and avoids you from going back and forth or otherwise introducing elements that are later forgotten about because you are not clear and focused on what you are writing. Having a major plot point in each section ensures that each section is rich and your reader is engaged the entire time. This is ultimately the structure you need in order to draw your reader forward and keep them moving through the story until they reach the end.

Chapter 3: Developing Your Story

Now that you are aware of what it takes to design a strong story structure, you may be wondering how you can develop a story that will fit with the structure! If you already have a general idea, then you can use the information from this section to help you strengthen that idea and ensure that all areas of your story are considered before them being structured and then written. If you have no idea as to what your story is going to be yet, use this chapter to help you identify a story and develop it so that it provides you with plenty of material to write your book about.

Study Existing Plots

When you are working towards developing your story one of the best ways to go about it is to read. Reading other people's stories gives you the opportunity to see what worked and what didn't, and it also provides you with inspiration to enrich your own story. While you don't want to be plagiarizing or stealing stories from other people, getting inspiration to enrich your own and strengthen the plot is always a great idea. This ensures that you are going to have a really strong story that provides enough material to engage your audience and keep them captive for the duration of the book.

When you are studying other people's stories you want to do more than just read them. You want to pay attention to who the characters are, how they develop throughout the novel, how the events take place including when and where, and all locations that the story takes place in. You should also identify the sequence that the locations are used in. Knowing more about these primary areas of the story allows you to get an idea of how books are written and what authors do in order to develop their own storyline. You can see the techniques in action and understand how they contribute to the overall experience being delivered in the story.

Draft Up Your Plot

When you are designing your plot there are some strategies you can use to see your plot come together without writing out the entire story first. The best way to do this is through drafting up your plot. You can do this by writing a paragraph or two from each ideal chapter and then read them in order. While it will obviously be missing many details, doing this will give you an idea of how the plot points flow together and if they are strong enough to give you plenty of writing material to work with.

Using a plotting strategy like this gives you the opportunity to look at your plot as a whole and make sure that it works effectively in the story you are writing. This helps you see what areas of the plot are rich and which aren't. You can also finalize the main plot sequencing and points before starting the writing process so that you are certain that it is in the order that you want and that it all works well together. This essentially gives you a birds-eye view of what your structure is and lets you know whether or not it works.

Create a Timeline

A great way to build your story is to create a timeline. This timeline should include all of the major plot points in chronological order. Seeing these together helps you identify how each one builds into the next one and makes sure that they work well together. If anything is missing or you feel there is a plot point that does not fit well in the overall story, then you can use this as an opportunity to eliminate it.

Similar to drafting your plot, creating a timeline allows you to take a birds-eye view at the work you have created and determine whether or not it works. The more you pay attention to the structure of your story from different elements now, the more you can be certain that it will work and produce a strong story in the long run.

Plan Character Development Along the Plot Line

After you have generated your plot draft and your timeline, take your characters into consideration. Pay attention to how you want them to develop along the storyline. It is natural for characters to change throughout stories, and even necessary in order for the story to progress. A great way to plan their development is to plan it alongside the story development. How is the development of the story going to contribute to the growth of the character? Consider this while you are deciding how your character will develop along the way.

Change the 5 "W's

A great way to ensure that you have developed the story strong enough is to check that you have changed the five w's along the way. The who, what, when, where, and why of the story should all develop or completely change along the progression of your story. In real life, these change from moment to moment and day to day. If you want your story to be realistic and relatable, you need to ensure that they are changed in your story as well.

If you want to take your story from good to great, these answers should not be simple and direct. Each one should have a series of answers that guide the element from the start of the book to the end. They should change in a way that convinces the reader that the change was natural and realistic, and helps the character feel as though it is a true story being told. Think back to your own day, for example you may have woken up in your home and now you are sitting in a coffee shop reading this book. You may have woken in a bad mood and now you are in a better one, or vice versa. The reasons as to why your mood change are also important to the story of your day. Who was involved in your day and what helped you pass the day by will have also changed from moment to moment. Just like your day naturally progressed as a story of its own, you need your story to progress in the same way. This ensures that your book goes in-depth enough to make it convincing to your reader. If any of the five w's are not developed enough, look for opportunities to strengthen them so that your story will be rich and full of realistic details.

Design a Story Board

Creating a storyboard is another great way to look at the structure of your story. A great way to create the storyboard is to write each major plot point and important element on a cue card or post it so that they can easily be moved around to create the final story map. This gives you a great opportunity to see how each event works together and organize them effortlessly without having to scratch out things and replace them everywhere.

Consider Subplots

Creating subplots that fit in seamlessly with your overall story is a great way to enrich the story experience and add more depth to it while also encouraging reader engagement. Subplots are essentially the "what else" part of the story. For example, if you are writing a book about the main character who is seeking justice, consider including elements of why this justice is so important for this character. Perhaps they want the criminal incarcerated because he or she deserves to be, but it may also be because the protagonist has allowed others to walk all over him for too long and he is ready to stand up for himself. Therefore, getting justice is both about having justice served *and* about building the confidence to actually fight for what is right.

Subplots are an incredible story developing strategy that can help you create a story that is much richer in context. You can include as many or as few subplots as you want, but make sure that each one makes sense to the overall story itself. They should work together with the main plot, rather than going against it or straying away from it completely.

Incorporate Driven Elements

All of the best stories incorporate one specific element that enables the story to be so great. That is the element of change. In order to create change, there are two very specific things you need. Character-driven and action-driven elements to your story. These elements are two things that can help incorporate change into your story in such a way that yours fosters all of the greatness that all of the other best titles do.

The reason why change is so powerful in a story is that that is what drives the story forward. People are curious to know about how characters change and grow throughout the course of the story every bit as much as they are interested in learning about how the story develops itself. People do not want to read a story about static characters who do the same thing every day and nothing changes. That would be extremely boring and would lead to them closing the book and turning away from it entirely. Think about it, would you read a book like that? Likewise, people are not interested in a book that has minimal change, or where the change only occurs on one very specific thing. Instead, people want to see the entire story change. They want to see the characters grow, they want to see the circumstances evolve, and they want to see the protagonist, and even the antagonist, end up somewhere completely different from where they were when the story changed. Incorporating as much natural and realistic change as possible helps drive your story forward and keep it both interesting and engaging.

As previously mentioned, there are two different types of change you can use to drive your story forward: character-driven change, and action-driven change. Both of these elements should be included in your own story if you want a diverse and realistic story that will help keep your readers engaged and reading your book all the way until the last page.

Character-driven change is used by showing the stakes the character has. For example, their child, their family, their significant other, their career. By incorporating these stakes and giving the reader insight as to why they are so important to the character, you can use them as an opportunity to drive the story forward. The most important thing to understand is that without character-driven change, there is no story. Character-driven change is essentially the answer to "why" your character is doing anything that takes place in the story. This explains why they will do almost anything, even stuff that seems highly irrational or nonsensical, in various situations. "Because my child is sick" or, "because I could lose my job" for example, would be the stakes and therefore would answer "why" the character is so invested in something. By creating this type of explanation and therefore emotional attachment from the reader to the character, and furthermore the character's stakes, you can make virtually every part of the story that much more engaging and interesting for your reader. Without character-driven change, your readers are not given an opportunity to understand why they need to care about the events taking place in your book.

Action-driven change is an entirely different form of change. This is the change whereby specific actions happen that cause the story to drive forward. High-speed chases, break-ins, getting arrested, being put on the chopping block at work, the spouse falling in love with someone else, the kid getting into trouble, all of these would constitute as action-drive changes. For the most part, these are actions that are taking place that cannot be stopped or influenced by your protagonist. Instead, the protagonist must find a way to respond and react to these actions.

When you use character-driven change effectively, action-driven change becomes that much more intriguing and engaging for your reader. Because they understand the stakes and have developed an emotional attachment to your characters, they are much more concerned with the action, as well as the outcome. It is important that you use a balanced amount of both types of changes in your story. This will help you round out your story and keep it moving forward without being too heavily charged in one direction or another. Furthermore, you want to make sure that you don't go overboard on the change. While it does drive the story forward, you want to make sure that you use it in a very realistic and natural manner. This helps the reader relate to the story and believe it, instead of feeling as though it is completely unlikely and therefore it is not relatable. If a reader cannot relate to a story in one way or another, they are not going to continue reading it because it will be too unbelievable for them.

Question Yourself

When you are in the process of developing your story, make sure you question yourself a lot along the way. The more you question yourself, your intentions, the story and the plot line, the more you can develop it. Questioning it ultimately gives you the opportunity to see where any loopholes may lie, if any part of the plot is weak, or if there is any reason that you should need to develop part of the story more. It also helps you identify where there may be too much action or development going on so that you can scale it back. If you are not taking the time to question yourself and your story structure, you may be missing important things that could take away from the value of your story altogether.

Some great questions to ask yourself include ones such as:

- Why has the character changed, how did the change happen, and what was the purpose of this change?

- How much has the character changed since the beginning of the story?

- Is the change natural and believable?

- What has each plot point taught the characters, thus teaching them about the story's primary situation or conflict?

- Can you identify some core themes within' the story? Are there too many or too few core themes taking place?

- Is the story believable? Does it flow naturally?

- Does the story move forward effectively, or is it too slow?

Asking yourself these questions will help ensure that each part of your story structure is strong and that it will help you produce a believable, relatable, and enjoyable story that is interesting and engaging. If you find that your answer is "no" or "I don't know" to any of the questions above, take the time to further explore that question and find ways that you can strengthen the story structure itself.

Get Feedback

Finally, it is important that you take the time to get feedback on your story structure. As with most things, having someone else take a look and give you some insight as to where the strengths and weaknesses lie and if any adaptations or alterations should be made means that nothing will be missed. This is the best way to make sure that you have a strong structure going into your story that will both serve you and serve your readers by giving you enough material and answers to generate an interesting an engaging story.

If you do not personally know someone who can provide you with feedback, there are many online platforms and forums that you can turn to where you can find someone to help you with looking over the structure. Furthermore, you can also look to find someone from your ideal target audience and have them look over the structure for you. Regardless of who you get to help you with the structure, do your best to make sure it is someone who is either in or thoroughly understands your target audience, and ideally someone with some experience in story structure. Having someone who intimately knows you are trying to reach and what you are trying to say can help significantly as it ensures that any feedback or critique they provide you with is accurate and helpful. Those who are unclear on the audience you are trying to reach or who have zero understanding of story structure or what is required in order to make a good book may not be able to provide you with information that will help you improve your structure. In fact, they may even have you questioning parts that you should not need to question. It is important that the person you choose to work with understands your needs.

Chapter 4: Creating Suspense

Regardless of what genre you are writing for, you need to be skilled in creating suspense for your story. Suspense is the element that keeps readers wondering what is coming next and how events are going to unfold. When used properly, suspense can be what draws one plot point to the next. If you want to create a compelling and convincing fiction novel that encourages readers to continue reading, you are going to need to master the art of creating suspense. The next ten tips are about how you can begin creating suspense in your own novel to keep your readers wanting more.

Understand Your Genre

Before you begin creating suspense, it is important that you understand the genre you are writing in. Each genre uses suspense differently to draw characters forward and keep readers coming back. If you want to do your book justice, you need to practice using suspense for your unique genre.

Let's take a look at three different types of novels and where the suspense would come into play for each type.

Mystery: A horror or major event takes place in the first chapter and the rest of the book is spent figuring out why the event occurred and who was responsible for it. For example, the protagonist's spouse was killed in the first chapter and the rest of the book is spent uncovering who was responsible.

Romance: You build up to the point where the two lovers finally get together. The climax, or the two getting together, officially takes place later in the book, usually within' the last couple of chapters. For example, two lovers know they're meant to be together but the timing never seems right. One is always dating someone else when the other is available for the relationship to work. As a result, they are never able to get together until the end when they finally make it work.

Suspense: The knowledge of an impending horror is upon the characters in the novel and they spend the entire time trying to avoid it until they can no longer keep it from happening. For example, someone knows they are going to jail for embezzlement but doesn't know when. This character knows that he has been tracked and that the FBI is well aware of what has been going on. He does not know when he will be taken down, but it will happen.

Provide Adequate Viewpoints

When it comes to developing a strong case of suspense in your novel, you need to give the reader adequate knowledge. This comes from providing them with different viewpoints. Through this, you can give them insight to the protagonist's side of things, and the antagonist's side of things. The best way to get a lot of suspense building in your book is by giving your reader insight as to what is going to happen before the protagonist knows. This gives the writer the opportunity to increase the emotional attachment to the protagonist and the stakes. The reader is drawn along an experience where they know what is yet to come but they have to watch the protagonist find out and learn the consequences of certain actions. The tension that builds on the reader because of what they know that the protagonist doesn't know is similar to someone who has a secret they're not allowed to tell. It engages the reader and makes them want to know more and to understand where the book will end up.

Put Time on Your Side

Time is an incredible tool when it comes to writing a book with suspense. You want to use time on your side so that you can increase the amount of suspense in the novel. Time gives you the opportunity to make the reader feel as though the protagonist is working against the clock. Everything they are doing should have some form of time constraint on it. Ideally, it should appear as though the clock is working in favor of the antagonist or antagonistic force to keep the suspense strong. For example, if you were writing a mystery novel about a murder that took place, it should seem as though the protagonist doesn't have enough time to find the murderer. Perhaps there is some jurisdiction law that states that if the person is not found within' a set amount of time the charges won't be as strong, or the murderer has been leaving clues that they have left town and it gets harder and harder to find who they are. Several dead end leads are exhausted before the protagonist finally discovers who the murderer was in the end. Putting time on your side lets you build suspense by creating the illusion that something won't happen, even though it needs to.

Keep The Stakes High

The stakes that you use in a story should be high enough to justify a high amount of suspense. The higher the stakes the more pressing the need to protect them is, both in the mind of the character and the reader. While you don't need to choose devastating stakes that are excessively high, picking ones that someone would actually be desperate to protect will ensure that your reader understands why the protagonist is so passionate about protecting their stakes. Some examples would include an executive who is facing being exposed for shady business dealings, therefore costing them their job and their reputation and making them unlikeable for other employers. Or, perhaps a male is in love with a female in a romance novel, but he grows tired of waiting for her to make up her mind so he pursues a relationship with someone else. She realizes she wants him more than anything but must figure out a way to tell him, and fast, before he marries the other person or realizes that he does not want to be with her altogether. Alternatively, you may choose to write a story about someone with a powerful societal position being murdered and they must find out who did it before they strike another powerful member of society. By keeping the stakes high but reasonable, you make it very clear as to why your reader needs to be so concerned with what is taking place in the book. The stronger your stakes are, the more your reader will be passionate alongside your character to ensure that they are not lost.

Don't Be Afraid to Apply Pressure

Pressure is a great way to add suspense to any novel. The odds should be stacked well against your character and it should take a great amount of effort and energy for them to tip the odds in their favor and save the day. The more the odds are stacked against them, the higher the pressure is and therefore the more you can draw the reader to wondering if they will ever be able to beat the odds. When they finally do, the reader and character alike will feel a great deal of relief from the experience.

When you are writing about creating pressure, make sure that you never lead your protagonist right to the breaking point. They should bend and cripple under pressure, but they should never stop pushing. You should ensure that they are always pushed *almost* too far so that they have *just* enough amount of energy to push back and it is at that time that they finally beat the antagonistic force and experience success in their heroic attempts.

Make Use of Dilemmas

Dilemmas are a great way to increase suspense in a story and have your reader highly engaged. Dilemmas present a "this or that" action for the character. They should be forced into action, and make sure that the pressure is on for it to happen fast. When dilemmas are being thrown towards your character it is important to make sure that they are being thrown by the antagonist most often. This should present the idea that the protagonist cannot win in the situation. For example, for them to save one character another must die, they can either lose their family and save their job or lose their job and save their family, or even indulging in alcohol after swearing to sobriety at some point within' the novel.

When you are presenting dilemmas, make sure that the antagonist always crosses the line. Because they are the villain, they shouldn't even think twice about going across it. However, the protagonist should always be forced with their morals and values. Should they do one, or the other? Which will be the less of two evils? Is there a way that they can make the best of both horrible situations? True to heroic nature, they should be struggling to find the answer to the dilemma.

One great reason why dilemmas work is because you can apply pressure and time constraints so that the protagonist is forced to make a decision fast, which puts pressure on him and gets the reader worried about what is going to happen. Using these three strategies together is a great way to build suspense throughout your book.

Complicate Things

You don't need to restrict to just presenting your protagonist with one or even two conflicts at any given time. Instead, feel free to pile on the complications every now and again. The more complicated things get, the more difficult it will be for them to come up with the solution and make the right choice. At times, it should feel like the protagonist is trying to juggle several balls at once and he is just barely keeping them from dropping every time. This is a great time to push the protagonist almost to the point of breaking before bringing them back in for a final and much awaited victory.

Avoid Becoming Predictable

When your book runs too smoothly, it becomes predictable. It also becomes uninteresting and the readers struggle to relate to it. Life is not about being smooth and predictable. Most often we are all living in a hot mess where we are balancing many different things and trying to stay afloat along the way. If you want to write a great book, it should be similar to this. Throw random curveballs in, take a spin somewhere where one wasn't expected, and have your reader surprised at some of the elements that are being tossed in, and when. When it comes to writing, don't let the hero rely on the idea that everything will go in their favor. In fact, almost nothing should. This way when it finally does, it will come as a surprise. Furthermore, your antagonist shouldn't go with everything going in their way, either. Let both of them face challenges, twists and turns along the way. The more they are affected by curveballs and unexpected experiences, the more realistic the story will be. Make the protagonist slip up and result in an almost-victory instead of a true victory, and let the antagonist fail at the most inconvenient of times for them. This keeps your readers on their toes and unsure about what is going to happen, when.

Develop Your Villain

Your villain is the antagonistic force in your book, and they need to be developed really well. Your reader should be mentally pushing against the villain, and rooting for the hero. As a result, you need to have a really well developed villain that has the reader truly believing and feeling as though they are a nasty force to be reckoned with.

Make sure that you use the right villain for your novel genre, as well. In a mystery, for example, it should not be clear as to who the villain is until the end. With a romance novel on the other hand, the villain might be time itself, or the person coming between the two lovers and keeping them apart. Alternatively, in a suspense novel the villain should be highly visible at all times and people should ultimately just be wondering when they will finally strike. The more you understand what type of villain is appropriate for your unique genre, the easier it will be to create one that is believable and extremely well developed.

When you develop your antagonist, make sure that you are very specific on who they are and what makes them tick. You want this character to be so developed that your reader feels as though they personally know them. Furthermore, your antagonist should change throughout the story, which is easiest to prove if your reader knows who they are from how you've written about them.

Develop Your Hero

In addition to developing your villain, you need to develop your hero. This is the one that finally defeats the antagonistic force and creates the victory of the story. The best way to create a strong hero is to really build on the character and give the reader plenty of reasons to love them. This is the character your reader is going to follow throughout the story. This is who they will be rooting for, worrying for, and curious about. They want to know everything they can about this character, and they have mentally prepared themselves to be on their side emotionally. Therefore, you need to use this character to not only build an emotional attachment between your reader and your protagonist, but also to use that attachment to manipulate the emotions of your reader. The protagonist is the character that you are going to leverage in order to get your reader nervous, curious, excited, happy, sad, angry, and any other emotion you want them to engage in throughout the experience. The best way to do that is to have a well-developed character that your reader can truly feel as though they have befriended.

Chapter 5: Additional Story Structure Tips

In addition to tips on basic story structure, developing a strong story, and how to create suspense, there are many other great tips that can help you when it comes to story structures. Now that you have the three important elements down, you can explore additional tips that will take you further into the realm of pro writer and help you generate a story that is going to be fantastic. The following tips are provided from real authors who have experience in writing their own high quality fiction materials. By following these tips, you can ensure that you don't only have a great story structure, but a phenomenal one.

Research Different Story Structures

Although there is a basic system that virtually all structures follow, it is important to understand that there are many modifications and alterations made to this structure in true writing. After all, if every story followed the basic structure down to the last detail then there would be no point in reading. We would be able to read the first chapter and know exactly how a book was going to turn out. By making modifications to the structure and playing it around in different ways, writers have the ability to stick to a structure that works while also providing a script that is unique, unpredictable, and engaging for readers.

Armed with this knowledge, you can prepare yourself to start researching many different story structures. The best way is to read other people's novels and do your best to identify the structure within' them. As you are reading, write down the major plot points and other key details that come into play with these plot points. Doing this will help you identify a series of structures that are used to create incredible novels, and how the writers spun them to work for the story. Do this several times over and pay attention to patterns that arise. Then, choose the structure you like most and make it work for your novel!

Stick to Structures that Are Traditional for Your Genre

For the best results, it is important that you stick to structures that are traditional to your genre. Although this may sound like a surefire way to create a story that sounds like every other story in the genre, it actually isn't. You will learn more about why in a moment. In the meantime, it is important that you understand why it is a good idea to stick to these traditional structures.

Each structure is designed to create a different effect for the story. Some build suspense, some build mystery, and some build both. Depending on what genre you are writing for, you are going to want to go for a structure that provides you with the right elements of virtually everything. These are going to be elements of suspense, story building opportunities, character development opportunities, and more. Each genre tends to be told in a unique way because it achieves a specific result. Therefore, each structure that is unique to each genre is built to help achieve that specific result. For example, you wouldn't want to use a suspense structure for a mystery novel because you would thus be identifying the perpetrator immediately. Likewise, you wouldn't want to use a mystery structure in a suspense novel because it would destroy the element of suspense by not giving enough information to the reader.

It is important that you do not reinvent the wheel, but rather you explore the different styles of wheels that exist for your market. Furthermore, just because you are limited to only using structures that are traditional for your genre does not mean that there is only one single structure you can follow. Each genre has its own selection of structures that will and won't work. The best way to identify which one you want to use is to read them, as described in the previous section, and pay attention to each type of structure you come across. As you do, identify which one would work best for your unique story and enlist that as your structure of choice.

Structure the Novel to Your Central Theme

As you are designing the structure for your novel, make sure that you are conforming the structure to fit the central theme of your novel and not the other way around. You never want to be derailing or detracting from the story as an attempt to stick to your structure. Remember, a structure is supposed to be a guideline that gets you to where you need to go. You do not have to follow it down to every last detail in order for your story to be a good one. Instead, you want to pay attention to the story structure and write your novel with that structure in mind.

Stories that are written to strictly to the guidelines set out in the structure end up sounding very forced and uncomfortable. Readers will often lose engagement quickly because the story becomes predictable and unnatural. They cannot relate to the story so they do not want to read it any longer. Ultimately, it takes away from the reader's experiences and kills the chance of your novel being greater.

To elaborate on how the structure *should* be used, we will explore how exactly you can enforce its guidelines. One of the biggest things you want to pay attention to, and use your structure for, is to ensure that your book stays focused on the central theme. If your novel strays too far away from the central theme at any given point, it may take away from the story overall. You never want to over share or get off track on a topic that does not contribute to the central theme or purpose of your novel. This is where your story structure comes in handy. Having a structure that can help keep you on track is highly valuable as it ensures that you do not derail your story and end up with a novel about love that gets too off track and ends up being about one person's career, or something else. Essentially you want to employ your story structure as a guide to keep you on track and to build a strong story, but you do not want to follow it so closely that you snuff out the quality of your story and produce something generic and predictable.

Modify the Template to Suit Your Plot

To expand further on the previous tip, it is important to work on modifying your template to suit your plot. Although you do not want to create an entirely new structure for your novel, or take one from the wrong genre, this does not mean that you cannot modify the template. For example, if you would prefer a certain plot point to happen sooner rather than later, or vice versa, you certainly have creative freedom to make this decision. Remember, you are a storyteller and your story is your work of art. Just because there are certain methods to use doesn't mean you can't get creative. For example, paint brushes are what you are *supposed* to paint with, but many choose to paint with sponges or even rags instead. Some even use a different material altogether, and yet the art is still incredible beautiful. In fact, it may be even more beautiful because of the unique method used. In this analogy, a different approach was used but the same bare basic structure was used: a tool was used to pick up paint and apply it to a canvas. You can easily modify certain parts of that, such as by changing your tools or picking a unique canvas, but at the very root is the same structure. The same goes for writing.

Just because authors before you have always used a specific template doesn't mean you cannot modify that template to suit your story. If you find that certain elements would serve better at a different area in the story, you are always welcome to do that. The best thing you can do as a writer is exercise your creative freedom. When you let loose from expectations and open yourself up to generate phenomenal content, inevitably you generate phenomenal content. As long as you stick to the bare bones basics with your structure, you are going to end up with a great story. If on the off chance you don't, it is a great opportunity to further research the structure and understand where you went wrong and how you could create a better story and structure in the future.

Create the Structure First, Modify it Later

It is always a good idea to begin your story with a strong structure. That being said, you should seek to create the structure before you begin writing. Having your structure created first and then creating a story around that structure helps ensure that you are staying on track with the basics. However, that does not mean that you are restricted to only writing to that specific structure.

As writers carry along the process of writing, they often find that it takes them down a natural path and therefore certain elements of their original structure no longer serve the story as powerfully as they could. The best thing to do in this circumstances is to reevaluate the structure and modify it so that it better suits the story in the direction that you have taken it. When you do this, you open yourself up to the opportunity of creating something much more powerful than you originally set out to do.

Creating a story is not always as straightforward as it seems. In many cases you will go into it with a very specific idea of what you want the story to be like and as a result of your writing process you discover that it actually works for reasons other than you thought so it naturally evolves away from your initial intentions. The best thing you can do in these circumstances is honor that natural evolution in your story and work with it. If you try and go against it in order to stick to your original structure you may end up creating a strange and unnatural twist backward, or it will otherwise not flow well. In order to give yourself creative freedom while also holding on to some sense of direction, the best thing to do is to start with a structure and modify it if your story evolves away from the initial structure you laid out for it. This will keep you on track while also giving you the potential to create an incredible story.

Hide the Structure in Your Writing

When it comes to the writing process, you want to ensure that you are hiding the structure within' your writing. It should not be painfully obvious what structure you have used. If it is, then your story will become predictable and people will lose interest. Virtually every story structure has been used several times over. This means that people will have a pretty easy ability to link your strategies together and determine what the novel will end like regardless of whether or not they have read it. They will also likely discover what major plot points are going to occur well before they ever happen. When the book becomes this predictable, it also becomes highly uninteresting.

A great writer knows how to hide the structure within' the story. Make things happen sooner or later than expected, twist away from the structure here and there to blend it in, and do your best to avoid going very clearly from point one to point two. You want your readers to question what is happening and be surprised along the way. Give them the idea that they have already arrived at the major plot point with one activity and then blow them out of the water with something much bigger. Keep the element of surprise active and use it as your weapon to bury the structure. The less obvious your structure is, the more unpredictable your story becomes and therefore the more power you have as the author to keep your reader engaged and have them wanting to learn more about what you have yet to tell them.

Keep Your Structure Organized and Handy

For a practical writing tip in regards to your structure, it is important that you keep it organized and that it is available at all times when you are writing. Your structure will prove to be a highly valuable tool when it comes to producing your novel. Being able to refer back to it at different points and identify where you are at will help you know where to go with your story, as well as help you stay focused on the central theme and overall purpose of your book.

A great way to keep your structure handy and useful during the writing process is to have it written down somewhere, such as on cue cards, and nearby whenever you are writing. This way you can identify where you have already been on the structure and where you have yet to go. It will also provide you with the ability to refer back to it regularly, as well as effortlessly revise it as needed. The reason why you might want to make your "final" structure on cue cards is because if you choose to modify it along the way you can easily do it without having to completely start over or rewrite it. This makes it effortless for you to modify it as needed and keep the parts you want.

Experiment

There is nothing more valuable than hands-on practice when it comes to any hobby, and this fact is not lost on writing. If you are looking for an opportunity to create an incredible book, take any chance you have to experiment. There are many ways that you can experiment when it comes to writing, and each can help you increase your understanding of story structures and how they work into the overall book, as well as how you can use your unique writing style to make the most of your story structure.

One great method is to take note of a few different story structures that will work effectively for the genre you are writing in and then draft your story out based on these. This means that you want to write a few paragraphs on each part of the structure and then read them together. It will give you the opportunity to see how your story would work together and if you have generated a strong enough story structure for your book. Another method is to practice writing short stories with different structures in a smaller way. While you won't be able to pack as much into the story as you would with a novel, it will give you a better idea of how your novel would sound with each unique structure in place.

Experimentation is the best way to practice writing and get an idea for what you like and what you don't like. If you are serious about it and you have time, practicing writing each novel with different structures and employing different strategies is a great way to see each structure in action and get a feel for how it works for your books. You can identify how the structure serves your story and where it might be weak, as well as how you can embed the structure within' the story using unique writing strategies to hide it from plain sight. This is a great way to practice writing overall and increase your skill if you are interested and have the time to invest.

Take Notes

Finally, a great method to use when it comes to learning and growing as a writer or as virtually anything is to take notes. When you are reading other books, take notes on what you like and don't like about the book, particularly when it comes to the structure of the book. When you are writing your own books, pay attention to where you have struggled and where you are succeeding. On the points where you a struggling, explore ways that you could make it easier. When it comes to each unique structure, write down how it serves your story and any thoughts you might have about how it could be better next time, or when you go through the editing process.

Taking notes allows you to review what you have already thought and felt about certain experiences with your story and its structure and gives you something easy and finite to look back on. When you take notes it means that you are not going to forget about or lose your thoughts in the process. This means that you can hold onto them and make the necessary changes without having to attempt to remember what it was that you wanted to do in the first place.

There are many great strategies you can use to strengthen your story structure immediately, as well as to help you increase your skills and become a better story writer through your structure over time. The more you emphasize on learning this skill now, the greater you will be at is as you go on. Remember that a strong structure can truly make or break a story. A bad structure equals a bad story, a good one equals a good story and a great structure will return you a great story. If you want to be great, you have to practice being great from the start. Over time and with practice you will graduate from being great to being phenomenal!

Conclusion

Thank you for reading *"Story Structure: Step-by-Step | Essential Story Building, Story Development and Suspense Writing Tricks Any Writer Can Learn"*. This book was designed to assist you in learning everything you need to know about story structures, including how you can make an incredible one.

I hope this book was able to elaborate on the concept of story structures, including what they are and why they are important. I also hope that you were able to learn plenty about how you can create your own story structure, develop your story, create suspense, and ultimately strengthen the structure of your story in order to create a phenomenal book.

The next step is to build your story structure and use it alongside the creation of your new book. Take your time and follow the steps within' this book to ensure that you have a strong structure that will serve you in the process of creating your book. Remember, as you go about the writing process you will want to check back to your structure to ensure that you are sticking to your original plan. However, if you find that your structure is no longer serving the overall creation of your story, you can always modify your structure for stronger impact. Sometimes the writing process can alter our plans and take us down a separate natural path. If this happens, ensure that you use the structure to support your story and the other way around.

Thank you!